# Departure, Return

Connor Elizabeth Muolo

This book is dedicated to Jesus Christ,

who will come soon,

and with whom all things are possible.

For the earnest expectation of the creature waiteth
for the manifestation of the sons of God.


Romans 8:19

But I would not have you to be ignorant, brethren, concerning them which are asleep, that ye sorrow not, even as others which have no hope.

For if we believe that Jesus died and rose again, even so them also which sleep in Jesus will God bring with him.

For this we say unto you by the word of the Lord, that we which are alive and remain unto the coming of the Lord shall not prevent them which are asleep.

For the Lord himself shall descend from heaven with a shout, with the voice of the archangel, and with the trump of God: and the dead in Christ shall rise first:

Then we which are alive and remain shall be caught up together with them in the clouds, to meet the Lord in the air: and so shall we ever be with theLord.

Wherefore comfort one another with these words.

I Thessalonians 5:13-18

But the day of the Lord will come as a thief in the night; in the which the heavens shall pass away with a great noise, and the elements shall melt with fervent heat, the earth also and the works that are therein shall be burned up.

Seeing then that all these things shall be dissolved, what manner of persons ought ye to be in all holy conversation and godliness,

Looking for and hasting unto the coming of the day of the God, wherein the heavens being on fire shall be dissolved, and the elements shall melt with fervent heat?

Nevertheless we, according to his promise, look for new heavens and a new earth, wherein dwelleth righteousness.

II Peter 3:10-13

# The Bud and The Bloom

The bud puts forth the
bloom,
And death follows.

It is beautiful,
Yet full of sorrow.

It blooms
To cast forth seed
For the earth
And for its own glory.

And though it dies,
It dies that others might
live.

So it is with the cross.

He was a seed planted,
To bloom in death,
That seeds of life
Could rain on the earth.

## My Heart Extols the Lord

*My heart extols the Lord*
There is myrrh in the love wherewith you have loved me,
The burial spice, the spice of sweet smell of love -
This duality.

It is easy to push you away.
I hear the Catholic Church shouting six blocks over in deep
voice,
And my upstairs neighbor is an old clock, striking the hours.
*My heart extols the Lord,*
*My heart extols the Lord,*
*My heart extols the Lord.*

You are not an object to remember.
You are not rain boots for the raining months.
You are not calculations of physics and school teachers' looks.

Can we just rest here for a while,
Thinking of myrrh and the duality.
To have life through death,
And in that moment you were someone that you never had been before...
*Eloi, Eloi, lama sabachthani?*

Violently, the flesh scattered to dry bones,
And you must have desired not to have come,
*Right?*

The without and the with God. Then the with and the without God.
*My heart extols the Lord.*

May I rest here for a while.
Reading your description of my teeth.
My scent, my hair, my eyes, my mouth, my temples, my neck -
They all ache for you.


Let me think of your face. I will read it.
I will write its lines in my heart.


You are all to me.
All of me is yours.
My scent, my hair, my eyes, my mouth, my temples, my neck.
All of me is yours.
*My heart extols the Lord.*


Putting you on, love letters love poems love books,
I am sick of love.


Gold, Frankincense, and Myrrh.
Lign Aloes, Myrrh, and white linen stitched in gold.

## The Glory

Hidden down in darkest cloister, depth of all the earth,
a Stone,
directed slowly upward through layers of time and story,
waited.

The Stone was defined, yet not,
sequestered mystery, definition down, dampened,
the mirror darkened.

Til one day, the ground divulged its Stone,
and water flowed, collected, and flowed still,
delving forth, directed into rivers fast and, dawning the new day,
life everlasting displayed.

Delight, oh my Desire, delight in the Stone,
dangerous and delicate, death's debt declared defeated,
dissolved, defunct.

The Stone upon which all stood and stands still,
discovered, dear.


Fall upon that Stone, oh all creation, and be broken.

## The Potter's Thumb

And the potter's thumb
reshapes the rim and the base.

The cup must first go through fierce heat
to see what the potter
had hoped across the pad of his thumb.

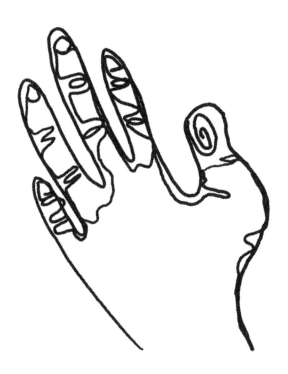

## I was Wrong (Spoiled)

I was wrong.

Thinking, surely if I give God my best,
Then he will give me the best he has to offer.

To me, that meant good grades and success.

It seemed the more I served God, the worse my
grades became,
Sinking like hopeful ships capsized on the way to
something else.

He's taught me this before, but I once again forgot.

It's hard to be below average, my pride whimpers at the head of the ship,
A sad little thud as it hits the ocean floor.
I can see sunk there all the little, sad idols peering up from the depths,
A bizarre graveyard to self-glory, self-fulfillment, self-pleasure, and the largest one:

self

I sacrifice to put you first, God, but then you hold it all back from me.

Where is the success that you write about in Joshua?
Where are all things in Matthew 27?
Where are the riches in Christ?
Where are all the blessings?

I didn't know that I believed in a prosperity gospel until all my prosperity left.

I understand that my thought process was wrong.

I understand now that to take up the cross means to walk all the way to Golgotha.

I understand now that to throw down one's life does not mean God's exaltation.

I understand now that "all these things" means the necessities of life and nothing more.

I understand now that "success" plays on a spiritual playing field, and that spiritual blessings in Christ are embraced against the chest of the inner man.

I understand that all this world could offer is just monopoly money lost in the cushions of the couch.

God is not a businessman trading stocks and sipping mimosas in a penthouse suite. He deals with the souls of men and walked in dust upon bare feet.

## Look in, Look Up

The long and shallow dip at the end of the road,
though still clay coffee and subterranean

(a brief water skimmer misplaced and thickened earthworms shadowed),

leads the soul to rejoice full of aching glory as the bright sky of arching clouds,
reflected across its willing surface,
shines bright blue and light.

Though the long, still pond holds no substance of things good,
and the slow passerby no more winks or nods in great redound

(still, yet still),

she holds characteristics of the celestial and vast
and reminds those going more slowly and more thoughtfully,
pondering the harder times or the hearts and souls of men, to look up.

look up

## Move Me Again - Time to Leave

And how much will I miss my table under the
embracing Lingonberry tree:

The sounds of
pianos and trombones and violinists and
clarinetists
floating through vinyl, laminated hallways.

Barefoot in hot grass.

Stalking city views from the quiet fourth floor of the library,
past the dear tapestry of thick, dry yarn draping down.

Storms rolling in from fifth floor walkways,
glass slides with fly eyes tinkling in a blue, or yellow, box.

So much learning.

Sleepless nights,
cracked deadlines in lead graphite,
and long pools under glass skylights that smell of tea tree oil.

Riding my bike at night alone and being chased off the road by cars passing by.

Tall, red brick home with terracotta roof and a small, sweet garden for peonies.
The secret home to mice droppings, bullet casings, raptured bikes,

and mad men banging at the door at 2 am.

I read all the signs of the end approaching.
Not as a thief in the night, but as an individual
with a metered time who blew a lot of it.

If this is what we know, five years and two degrees,

how much more should we do with what we don't know?

Sweet contentment with things of little worth:
0.7 pencils in an unopened bag,
owning all of Brookside on foot,
short ride to Crows on the trolley trail,
training in the park,
playing cricket in the street,
good words from good people,
learning to be alone in a city full of people,
learning to no longer be alone in a city full of people,
curry soup from coconut oil jars,
tuna from jam jars,
old tissues on old slides under old microscopes...

how much more contentment with things of
greater worth?

Passing the gospel, ear to ear, to find one faithful
man.

Faithful men are hard to find.

By faith, Abraham, when he was called to go out into a place which he should after
receive for an inheritance,
obeyed; and he went out, not knowing whither he went.


By faith he sojourned in the land of promise, as in a strange country,
dwelling in tabernacles with Isaac and Jacob,
the heirs with him of the same promise:
For he looked for a city which hath foundations, whose builder and maker is God.

I don't know where I am going, but I know where I am now.


You moved me once. Move me again.

# I'm Looking For You

I

The row of pink lines, round faces tousled at every frill and trill by the wind,
      finds its needs met in you.

II

The shorter friends, purple and yellow bunches
tossed not as much by the wind
as by the butterflies and bees
that leap and jump from their platforms - yes, these too,
the flowers and the bright flitting patterns under the sun,
      find their needs met in you.

III

The bright green old man finds his needs met in you
as he clings precipitously to a bright green stalk under pink shadows of round faces.
The stalks bend ever slightly with the wind,
and the old man could jump from long legs, but crawls on ponderously.
Yes, he finds his needs met in you.

IV

By the small pond, the grey turtle on the duck ramp finds his needs met in you,
and if we were to ask the somber-eyed feathered fowl,
they too would add their agreement as they shift weight over orange ankles.

V

The tall oak, though met suddenly with pain in the night,
a branch falling to the ground, loosened by the wind,
still stands taller than the sons of man,
pointing upward with the flowers, their faces all toward God above.
      She too finds her needs met in you.

VI

The tall girl seated on the stone pillar,
rough against her legs,
is tossed too by the wind with the tall oak and the tall stalks.
Though creased with care,
opening up to open outward before folding up to look inward,
and though life can be uncareful,
and though the broad winds and the fast winds and the cold winds
push and pull with many different voices,
she with all creation waits, face upturned, for the provision from your hand.

    And she finds her needs met in you.

## Lord, How Long?

Jerusalem.
The city of stone, of cold metals, and of sorrow.

Jerusalem.
The city of gold, of precious stones, and of pearls.
Joy eternal.

Set a watchman on her walls, O Lord.
Ha Messiah Y'shua came through that eastward gate, and it will be shut.
And though many tried to end the story there, it will continue
everlasting.

Rows of graves, open coffins aching,
and the shadows of trash fires at stone heads
will not stop him from returning again to Jerusalem.

Heads bowed against the wailing wall will lift up to the skies.
Small prayers written on folded papers tucked deep in stone cracks
will instead be carried by the Holy Spirit to Hasham.

Those who fear to speak his name shall call him Father in Jerusalem.

You are small and weak, Jerusalem, but Adonai is yours.
Those dead prophets sing in heaven, waiting.

Who will go to Jerusalem?

To Nazareth.
To Bethlehem of grey, steep streets.
To yellow, stoney Jericho.
To the careful and caustic West Banks.
To high Golan, where the wind whines up hard landscape.

Carmel is returned to shrines and idols.
Tel Aviv hides under gilding. Settlements crouch low and whisper.

Who will go to bring the gospel of peace?

## Patience

All these other things are all groaning and fuzzy sight,
the pinch of headache here where my brows frown
      and the red spider mite in conjunctiva.

...though now for a season, if need be,
Ye are in heaviness through manifold temptations...

      Listen! Let her do her work.
I roll my head back then snap right left,
vertebrae like tin cans sighing.
Ink on my fingers.
Patience, patience, beloved.

*Is this what you want from me?*

He promised me green grass where seven loaves are for thousands.
I turn my head and tinnitus turns to still waters
      and crickets and stars burning.
Patience, patience, it will come in time, don't worry.

My flesh faileth of fatness,
      but she works, more precious than gold.
Patience, patience, it will come in time, don't worry.
Patience, patience, beloved.

He is my Shepherd.
And though he slay me, yet will I follow him,
Whom having not seen, I love: in whom, though
now I see him not, I rejoice
      in him with joy unspeakable.
Patience, patience, beloved.

## When?

The clouds move across the sky through a reflection across a marble surface.
Words are like cameras.

They cannot capture the reality of thoughts and emotions.

All is quiet, and the Sun is still stretching forth.

Many are now waking up, and an eagle slides across the cool, slick marble.
The broad, cold of the sky separates me from you.

When will you call me up?
I too shall fly across reflections in cool marble.

My words cannot express how I feel.

An emotion sits in the depth of my yearning,
heavy across my bowels, yearning, sinking, lifting.


I write thoughts of you in a quiet, empty room.

And I look out the window to the rolling sky.

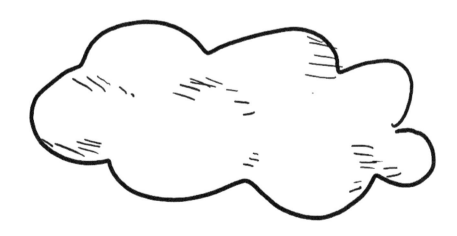

## Wait

When my mind is full of pathways of organs and rules of life,
my mind wanders to you.

When sitting above the street, watching bright beetles in straight lines,
my mind wanders to you.

When torn by words and thoughts in multitude,
my mind wanders to you.

When pressed beyond groanings and pricked in the most secret places,
my mind wanders to you.

That all paths lead to thoughts of your eternality, and that you ever were and ever
shall be, that you are beyond and far more and greater than all these,

my soul cannot find any of the proper words to describe.

I could not write it with ten years, nor could I find a place to pen it.
Nor could angels' voices find it.

But this I do know,
and even my smallest thoughts can
agree in long and drawn out words,
that my mind wanders to you.

And yours to me.

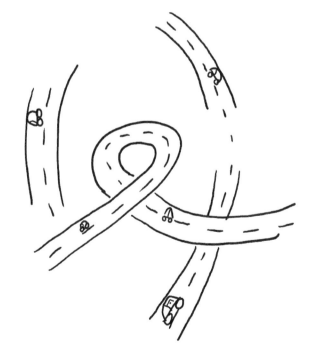

# Departure

In the autumn, the black crows call, call me to the long home,

The long home, which is not home to me, but only to half of me,

The flesh which will take on worms and soil

Though glorified if and when and at what time and where

He shall appear,

Appear to take me home to my long home,

A home with many rooms in one large house,

And God is next door.

How my heart breaks, and the crows call.


Red printed on leaves, ink prints of circulatory circuits,

The purple and red and brown and yellow and blue.


The black crows call, call me to the long home,

The long home, which is not home to me, but only to two thirds of me:

The soul which I am, the things I feel and felt and will, ever-living, feel.


The spirit, the breath of life from my Father.

Something borrowed, like the cold wall in the air in early mornings,

But it stays, most permanent and most graceful.

The flesh - that which walks but cannot see, is not in this long home.


The leaves drop, the trees cough and the air is full of paper.

All crushed to soft dust, all the same color in the streets.

Looking through panes of wrinkled glass at the fall of the sun,

Knowing that this night is long and not as smooth as velvet, (shadows lurk, and the leaves fall though no one sees),

Hearing the call of the crows, louder at the cusp of nightfall,

Trees neon beacons in the scattered peels of falling light,

My heart, in thirds, laughs and cries.


I hear the Catholic Church shouting six blocks over,

And my upstairs neighbor is an old clock, striking the hours.


Come soon, Lover.

Come soon, Father.

Come soon, Brother.

Come soon, Savior.


My flesh already in its long home in dark layers of old times,

Only an echo, a remnant of the past,

The fossils of spiral shell mollusks in silt and mud under swirling waters:

Those that once lived but no longer do.

Only I was still-born, and flesh is never alive.

It calls to the crows, the crows calling, calling it to the long home.


Come soon, Lover.

Come soon, Father.

Come soon, Brother.

Come soon, Savior.

The days are evil, the night is dark, my flesh is black and not as smooth as velvet.

The black crows call, call me to my long home.

Two long homes, split in twos, in thirds,

The neon trees blinking, the leaves falling, spilling thin ink to the earth.


Come soon, Lover.

Come soon, Father.

Come soon, Brother.

Come soon, Savior.

Come soon, One with me, my Wholeness.


Crows call, the leaves paper membranes I must also break through.

Aorta, Brachiocephalic, subclavian, auxiliary, ulnar, radial,

Fingers reaching out, reaching up, dropping leaves.

Even so, Come.

# Approaching

Summer is the time of remembrance.

To know what is coming in the cold winter,

To know what is past in the fresh spring.


New life passes away,

But the cold washes it all away,

Prepares the ground for the bulbs to spring up.

Cyclical.


To know one passing is to know rebirth.


Summer storms, twisting trunks, bark growling.

The cicadas bud from the ground and paint the air with song.


Bright light, sunbathing on old porches,

The warmth of a black dog's fur against your leg.

The children are all outside, and the pools laugh chlorine laughter

Until brief lightning calls it all off, and the trunks twist,

Bark growling.


When the earth melts its frost, does it know that it will freeze again?

To grow so brightly.

To love so simply.

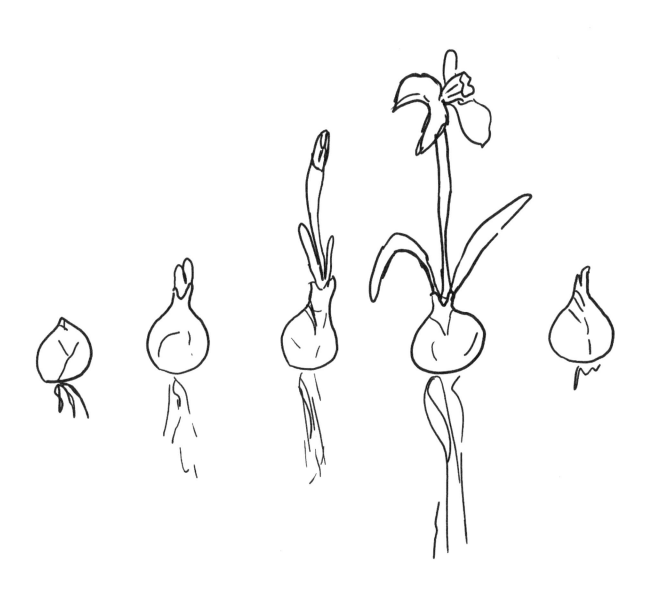

## Departure, Return

The God of true robin whistles, the sparrow ejecting collected rainwater from
overflowing gutters as it flutters and chirps.

Prickly pear spills across sidewalks, and the blocks flash cool shade to hot green
grass and leaves.

The departure seemed slow and aching, but the return seemed sudden:

first the tulips and irises peaking small heads up,
and then all the trees have blooms and buds,
and new leaves like soft hands collect golden light
like the blonde hair of toddlers and tykes.

All of this will be burnt up and poisoned.
Wormwood falls, and oceans and the moon to blood.

But you are just and righteous,
God, and you will again create.
And the departure was fast and slow, but the return is valiant.

There is no pain there, but there is pain here:

The drop of bee sting sweat, migraines at temples,
and dry chapped lips in a strong wind.

Sharp pricks and the nipping of pruning shears drawn red with rust and dirt,
dull, pulling but not cutting,
the bushes slapping back against the wall,
leaves and bees and small beetles bouncing on the soil,
a brick path laid atop seeds that will never grow for the weight and dark above.

An older man, collecting his newspaper on the brick path, trips and falls...

Speak softly, my soul.

He is very gentle. Soft velvet, rose petal leaves, and honey on

hurt

Rise up to sing, my soul.

He is a consuming fire. He shakes every corner of the

room

Rest, my soul.

He is near. I will be found in the cradle of his

hand

Joy, my soul.

He is my light. He turns my sighs into

                         Laughter

Lord, how long?

And what will be the sign of thy coming?

Please, Lamb, how long?
Will I be buried, or will I be raised?

Even so come. When?

You look on us, the deaf and the mute,

And you sigh.

You will come when you are done waiting.

CPSIA information can be obtained
at www.ICGtesting.com
Printed in the USA
BVHW092059180821
614616BV00016B/1118

9 781300 446309